The Greatest Bible Stories Ever Told
Children in the Bible

Stephen Elkins
AUTHOR

Tim O'Connor
ILLUSTRATIONS

BROADMAN
&HOLMAN
PUBLISHERS
NASHVILLE, TENNESSEE

BABY MOSES

Exodus 2:3   But when she could hide him no longer, she got a papyrus basket for him and coated it with tar and pitch. Then she placed the child in it and put it among the reeds along the bank of the Nile.

Many years later, after Joseph and all his brothers had died, Pharaoh was the new king of Egypt. He feared the children of Jacob, now called the Israelites.
"The Israelites are growing too strong," he said. "If there is a war, they may fight against us and defeat us."

To keep this from happening, he made the Israelites into slaves and put Egyptian masters over them. They were forced to work very hard making bricks and mortar.

Pharaoh used the bricks to build great cities. But no matter how unkind the Egyptian slave masters were, or how hard their work became, the Israelites continued to grow in number.

Pharaoh became so angry he passed a cruel law ordering every baby boy born to an Israelite family to be drowned in the Nile River.

Now it happened that a baby boy was born to an Israelite family. Fearing Pharaoh's decree, the mother hid the baby for months. But when he began to cry and move about, she had to do something to save him. She decided to make a large basket out of the reeds that grew near the river. She sealed it with sticky tar so it would float.

Then she put the baby in the basket and set it among the reeds along the riverbank. His sister, Miriam, stood at a distance to watch over the baby.

That evening, Pharaoh's daughter went down to the river to bathe. It was then she noticed the strange basket floating among the reeds. "Fetch that basket," she said to her servant girl. When she opened the basket and saw the little baby boy, she loved him.

Then Miriam came forth and said, "Would you like for me to get an Israelite woman to take care of the baby?" "Yes, I would," said the princess.

So Miriam ran back to get her mother and told her the things that had happened. "Take care of this baby and bring him back to me when he is older," the princess said.

When the child grew older, his mother took him to Pharaoh's palace, back to the princess, and he became her son. The princess named him Moses saying, "I drew him out of the water."

Affirmation: God will keep me safe!

ESAU AND JACOB:
THE TROUBLE WITH TWINS

Genesis 25:24   When the time came for her to give birth, there were twin boys in her womb.

Now Isaac loved the Lord and grew to be a great man of God. At age 40, he married a woman named Rebekah. Like Abraham and Sarah, they prayed that God would bless them with a child.

When Isaac was 60 years old, the Lord answered their prayers with a double blessing ... Rebekah was going to have twins! Even before the babies were born, Rebekah felt them kicking and fighting each other. "Why is this happening?" she asked the Lord.

8

The Lord answered and said, "Two nations are inside of you and the two will be separated. One will be stronger than the other; the older brother will serve the younger."

On the day of their birth, Esau, the first-born, was red and hairy. Jacob was fair and smooth and followed with his hand grasping Esau's heel. Just as Rebekah had been told, the two boys were very different. Esau grew up to be a very skillful hunter, while Jacob liked to stay close to home.

One day Esau came home weary and tired from a long day's hunt. Jacob had just finished cooking some tasty stew. Esau was very hungry when he said, "Jacob, let me have some of your stew." Jacob replied, "First, sell me your birthright."

This meant that Jacob, the second born, would have all the special honors given to the first-born.

Again, Jacob said, "Give me your birthright and I will give you food." Esau, being so tired and with the smell of Jacob's stew tempting him, replied, "I'm about to die anyway. What good is a birthright if you're dead of hunger? You can have it! Now, give me some stew!"

"Swear to me first," Jacob demanded.

So Esau swore before the Lord and gave Jacob his birthright. How foolish he was to sell his birthright for so little!

Many years passed and their father Isaac became very old and blind. Fearing he may die soon, he called for Esau and said, "Take your bow and arrow to the country and bring back some wild game. Prepare a meal just the way I like it and bring it to me. Then I will give you my blessing."

When Rebekah heard what Isaac had said to Esau, she called for Jacob. She told Jacob she had a plan to trick Isaac so that he would be the one to take the food to Isaac and receive the blessing. Jacob was concerned Isaac would know.

He said to his mother, "Esau is hairy and I

am not. What if father touches me and finds out I am not Esau? What if he curses me instead of blesses me?"

"The curse will be upon me," Rebekah said. "Now do as I tell you!" Then Jacob, dressed in Esau's clothes and with his hands covered with goat skins, took the meal into his father's room.

Jacob said, "The Lord God has given me a successful hunt. Rise and eat and give me your blessing." Isaac said, "Come close so I may touch you to know if you are really Esau." When Isaac touched the hairy goat skin hands and smelled Esau's clothes, he blessed him saying, "May all people bless and serve you. May nations bow down to you." Now Jacob had taken Esau's birthright and blessing.

Just as Jacob left his father's room, in came Esau with the tasty meal he had prepared for his father. "Rise and eat and give me your blessing," Esau said.

"Who are you?" Isaac asked. "I am your first-born son, Esau," he answered. Isaac trembled, "Who was it then that brought me food and received my blessing? For he will be blessed indeed."

When Esau heard his father's words, he cried, "Bless me, too, father, bless me, too!" Isaac raised his head and

said, "Your brother has deceived me. He has taken your blessing and I have made him lord over you and all his relatives. I can give you nothing."

Esau hated Jacob and said to all, "The day is coming when I will kill Jacob."

Affirmation: I will be a blessing to others!

13

CHILDREN OBEY YOUR PARENTS

Ephesians 6:1 Children, obey your parents in the Lord, for this is right.

Paul's letter to the church at Ephesus included some words just for children. Children, obey your parents in the Lord for this is right. Honor your father and mother which is the first commandment with a promise. God promises that things will be well with you and you will enjoy a long life on the earth.

Paul went on to explain that as followers of Jesus we are soldiers in the Lord's army. Satan is the enemy we fight.

So put on the whole armor of God. He gave these examples. Put on a *BELT OF TRUTH* and a *BREASTPLATE OF RIGHTEOUSNESS*. Cover your feet with the *GOSPEL OF PEACE*. Take up a *SHIELD OF FAITH* to protect you from Satan's fiery arrows. Put on a *HELMET OF SALVATION* and the *SWORD OF THE SPIRIT* which is the Bible. And pray about each decision and pray for your friends. Being a soldier isn't always fun, but God's army needs you every day to fight the good fight!

Affirmation: I am a soldier in the Lord's army!

THE EXAMPLE

1 Timothy 4:12 Let no one look down on your youthfulness ... Show yourself an example.

In a letter to his dear friend Timothy, Paul tells him to be about God's work, which is saving lost sinners. We are also to pray for the leaders of our country.

Then Paul writes some very important words, "For there is one God, and one peacemaker who stands between God and men; that man is Jesus Christ who gave Himself as a payment for our sin. This is the gospel message to young and old. Therefore, let no one look down on you because you are young; but rather set an example for those who believe."

Affirmation: I will set a good example!

JOSEPH: GOD PUT A DREAM IN MY HEART

Genesis 37:5 *Joseph had a dream, and when he told it to his brothers, they hated him.*

Some years later, Jacob married and had twelve sons. He settled in a place called Canaanland where his sons tended flocks of sheep.

Now Jacob had a favorite son named Joseph who was born when Jacob was very old. To show his great love, Jacob made Joseph a coat of many colors. Many times Joseph would come to his father and tell him the bad things his brothers were doing. This made his brothers very angry and jealous.

Joseph's brothers hated him for this and could not speak a kind word to him. One night the Lord sent Joseph a very special dream.

The next morning Joseph told his brothers all about it. He said, "We were in the fields tying bundles of grain together when suddenly my bundle rose up and stood tall while your bundles gathered around mine and bowed down to it."

"Do you think you will someday rule over us?" his brothers said. And they hated him even more.

Then Joseph had a second dream. He said to his brothers, "This time the sun, the moon, and eleven stars were bowing down to me." When he told the dream to his father, Jacob was very unhappy. "Do you believe that your mother, and I, and your eleven brothers will bow down before you?"

One day Jacob said to Joseph, "Your brothers are tending to our flocks near Shechem. Go to them and make sure all is well."

Joseph obeyed his father and soon found his brothers on a hillside. But his brothers had seen Joseph's coat of many colors from a distance, and before Joseph reached them, they plotted to kill him.

"Here comes the dreamer," they said. "Let's kill him and throw him into one of these empty water holes and say a wild animal attacked and killed him. That will put an end to his dreams!"

When the oldest brother Reuben heard their plan, he stopped it. "Do not kill him. Throw him into the pit, but do not harm him."

When Joseph saw his brothers, he ran to them. Suddenly, to his surprise, they all jumped on him and began tearing his coat of many colors from his back. They tied him up and threw him into an empty water hole.

As they sat to eat, a caravan bound for Egypt passed by. Judah spoke, "Why don't we sell Joseph to these merchants? Then we'll be rid of him forever!"

Joseph was sold as a slave to the merchants for twenty
pieces of silver. When Reuben found out what they
had done, he said, "How can we face our
father having done this?"

They decided to kill a young
goat and dip Joseph's coat
in the blood. They took
the coat to their father
and said, "Father we
found this coat on
our journey
back home.
Is it Joseph's?"

Jacob knew it was Joseph's coat and cried out, "It's Joseph's coat! Some wild animal has killed my son! He must have been torn to pieces."

Then Jacob tore his clothes and wept bitterly. No one was able to comfort him. Meanwhile, Joseph was on his way to Egypt.

Affirmation: I will not be jealous of others!

JOSIAH: A TEENAGER FINDS A TREASURE

2 Chronicles 7:14 If my people, who are called by my name, will humble themselves and pray ... I will hear from heaven and will forgive their sin and will heal their land.

When Josiah was eight years old, his father King Amon died making Josiah king. King Amon had disobeyed the Lord, as did his father King Manasseh. They worshiped idols, but Josiah loved the Lord God and sought to please Him in every way. So, while he was still very young, he destroyed the idols that were in Judah. Then he sent workers to repair the temple of the Lord.

While the workers were cleaning the temple, they found Israel's treasure. There in the dust was the Book of the Law written by Moses. It had been lost for many years. Shaphan, the scribe, took the scroll and ran to the palace. There he read the law to young King Josiah. The law warned Israel that if they disobeyed the commandments, God would send great trouble upon them. Josiah asked God for forgiveness for the way his people had sinned. He called all the people of Israel together and read the law and promised to obey it.

Affirmation: I will read my Bible each day!

FIVE LOAVES AND TWO FISH

Mark 6:41 And looking up to heaven, he gave thanks!

The news of Jesus' miracles began to
spread all over the land. People came to Jesus
from everywhere bringing Him their hurts
and sickness; and Jesus loved them ... every one!

But now He needed some rest. "Let us go to a quiet place,"
said Jesus. So they set sail across the lake. As they sailed
away, the people ran around the lake and were waiting for
them when they reached the other side.

When Jesus saw them, He loved them. They were like sheep without a shepherd; and after all, He was the Great Shepherd! So once again, He began teaching them and taking care of them.

It was late when the disciples said, "Jesus, send the people away so they can eat." But to their surprise He said, "You feed them."

"Feed them!" exclaimed the disciples. "That would cost too much!" Then Andrew spoke up. "There is a boy here with five loaves of bread and two fish. But how far will that go among so many?"

Then Jesus said, "Tell the people to sit down on the grass." As they were sitting down, Jesus took the five loaves and two fish and looked up into heaven. He thanked God and then began to break the loaves and fish into pieces.

Five thousand people were fed that day, and they all left with their bellies full. The disciples picked up twelve baskets full of bread and fish left behind by the crowd. Jesus has the power to supply all of our needs, no matter what!

Affirmation: Jesus will supply all my needs!

COLLECT ALL 10

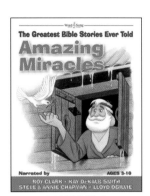

0-8054-2471-7

0-8054-2466-0

0-8054-2470-9

0-8054-2469-5

0-8054-2474-1

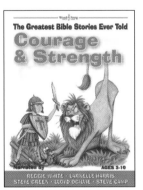

0-8054-2468-7

0-8054-2473-3

0-8054-2475-x

0-8054-2472-5

Available in Your Favorite Christian Bookstore.

0-8054-2467-9

We hope you enjoyed this Word & Song Storybook.